Emma Burgess

SUMMERSDALE

Copyright © Summersdale Publishers Ltd 2001

All rights reserved

No part of this book may be reproduced by any means, nor transmitted, nor translated into a machine language without the written permission of the publisher

Summersdale Publishers Ltd
46 West Street
Chichester
PO19 1RP

www.summersdale.com

ISBN 1 84024 178 0

Printed and bound in Great Britain

Text by Emma Burgess
Cartoons by Kate Taylor

You know you're a Maneater when ...

YOU KNOW YOU'RE A MANEATER WHEN . . .

You disapprove of people using the 'C' word: celibacy.

YOU KNOW YOU'RE A MANEATER WHEN . . .

Your New Year's resolution is to cut down to 20 a day, but you'll carry on smoking at full strength.

YOU KNOW YOU'RE A MANEATER WHEN . . .

YOU KNOW YOU'RE A MANEATER WHEN . . .

You are so horny that rhinos treat you as one of them.

YOU KNOW YOU'RE A MANEATER WHEN . . .

You celebrated your 16th birthday with a nostalgic look back to the night you lost your virginity.

YOU KNOW YOU'RE A MANEATER WHEN . . .

Stephen Spielberg would like to cast you as the predator in a *Jurassic Park* sequel.

YOU KNOW YOU'RE A MANEATER WHEN . . .

YOU KNOW YOU'RE A MANEATER WHEN . . .

Ann Summers nominated you as Customer of the Year.

YOU KNOW YOU'RE A MANEATER WHEN . . .

YOU KNOW YOU'RE A MANEATER WHEN . . .

You have a rugby team for breakfast...a few Sumo Wrestlers for lunch.
(That's just the starter.)
And the Army for supper.

YOU KNOW YOU'RE A MANEATER WHEN . . .

Grace Jones is scared of you.

YOU KNOW YOU'RE A MANEATER WHEN . . .

Your dentist finds bits of Y-front between your teeth.

YOU KNOW YOU'RE A MANEATER WHEN . . .

Contraceptive companies send a rep to visit you - you get through so many condoms, they think you're a chain of chemists.

YOU KNOW YOU'RE A MANEATER WHEN . . .

Your best chat up line is "grrrr".

YOU KNOW YOU'RE A MANEATER WHEN . . .

YOU KNOW YOU'RE A MANEATER WHEN . . .

Your friends think you should be kept in a zoo. They're not joking.

YOU KNOW YOU'RE A MANEATER WHEN . . .

Your celebrated your 18th birthday in bed with your boyfriends.

YOU KNOW YOU'RE A MANEATER WHEN . . .

YOU KNOW YOU'RE A MANEATER WHEN . . .

You can fit all your knickers into a matchbox.

YOU KNOW YOU'RE A MANEATER WHEN . . .

You have a higher sperm count than the most fertile of men.

YOU KNOW YOU'RE A MANEATER WHEN . . .

Your ex-boyfriend is convinced you learnt your mating techniques from watching too much *Wildlife on One*.

YOU KNOW YOU'RE A MANEATER WHEN . . .

You use a bus shelter for protection during sex.

YOU KNOW YOU'RE A MANEATER WHEN . . .

Marriage is a swear word.

YOU KNOW YOU'RE A MANEATER WHEN . . .

You don't just say 'come and get it'. More like 'wait there and I'll bring it to you!'.

YOU KNOW YOU'RE A MANEATER WHEN . . .

You heard that supermarkets are good pick-up joints and filled in a Tesco's job application form faster than you can orgasm.

YOU KNOW YOU'RE A MANEATER WHEN . . .

YOU KNOW YOU'RE A MANEATER WHEN . . .

You go home first thing in the morning.

YOU KNOW YOU'RE A MANEATER WHEN . . .

You're so accommodating you can hold more men than Chelsea Football Club.

YOU KNOW YOU'RE A MANEATER WHEN . . .

Your idea of a diet is having sex just once during the night.

YOU KNOW YOU'RE A MANEATER WHEN . . .

You think 'period pain' is so-named because it's a pain that it interferes with your sex life.

YOU KNOW YOU'RE A MANEATER WHEN . . .

Your ambition is to be a film star – porn films naturally.

YOU KNOW YOU'RE A MANEATER WHEN . . .

YOU KNOW YOU'RE A MANEATER WHEN . . .

You left home when your parents mentioned they were sending you to a convent school.

YOU KNOW YOU'RE A MANEATER WHEN . . .

Cystitis is a lifestyle.

YOU KNOW YOU'RE A MANEATER WHEN . . .

The bible you keep by your bed – *The Joy of Sex* – has been thumbed almost as much as you have.

YOU KNOW YOU'RE A MANEATER WHEN . . .

YOU KNOW YOU'RE A MANEATER WHEN . . .

Every pair of knickers you own has a different set of teeth marks.

YOU KNOW YOU'RE A MANEATER WHEN . . .

The condom vending machine in your bedroom is refilled more often than the one in your local pub.

YOU KNOW YOU'RE A MANEATER WHEN . . .

You don't know the meaning of the 'F' word: 'faithful'.

YOU KNOW YOU'RE A MANEATER WHEN . . .

Your doctor has told you to cut down your intake of fatty things, so you only sleep with athletes now.

YOU KNOW YOU'RE A MANEATER WHEN . . .

You have a surprising smattering of Latin in your vocabulary: *cunnilingus*, *fellatio* and *coitus interruptus*.

YOU KNOW YOU'RE A MANEATER WHEN . . .

Your French isn't too bad either, but it's a pity you can't count further than 69.

YOU KNOW YOU'RE A MANEATER WHEN . . .

You know more positions than a library of *Kama Sutras*.

YOU KNOW YOU'RE A MANEATER WHEN . . .

YOU KNOW YOU'RE A MANEATER WHEN . . .

The Chippendales demand a bodyguard when they're in your town.

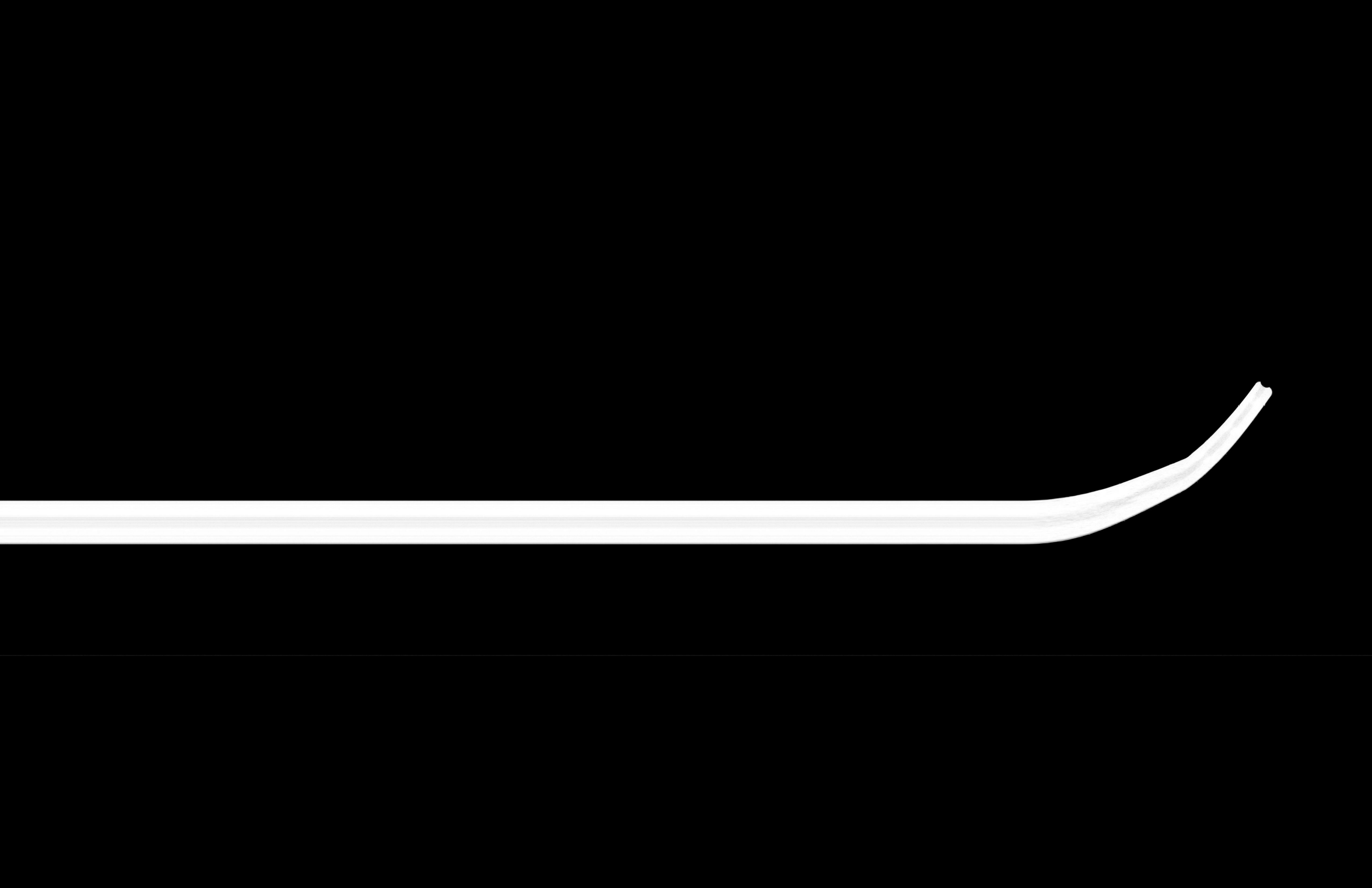

YOU KNOW YOU'RE A MANEATER WHEN . . .

You catch STDs more often than a commuter catches a train.

YOU KNOW YOU'RE A MANEATER WHEN . . .

Scientists used your DNA to formulate the drug *Viagra*.

YOU KNOW YOU'RE A MANEATER WHEN . . .

Your friends affectionately call you 'sperm bank' because so many men have left their deposits with you.

YOU KNOW YOU'RE A MANEATER WHEN . . .

Married women fear you.
Surprise surprise.

YOU KNOW YOU'RE A MANEATER WHEN . . .

So do divorced ones. You've probably just nicked their husband no. 2.

YOU KNOW YOU'RE A MANEATER WHEN . . .

A quiet night for you would be spent in front of the fire...romping naked with the blokes you've just picked up in the pub.

YOU KNOW YOU'RE A MANEATER WHEN . . .

YOU KNOW YOU'RE A MANEATER WHEN...

You are a modern day Houdini – you've found a way of having sex with even the most complicated chastity belt in place.

YOU KNOW YOU'RE A MANEATER WHEN . . .

Your friends all claim to have boyfriends and yet you've never met any of them. Weird, huh?

YOU KNOW YOU'RE A MANEATER WHEN . . .

You are prescribed the 'morning after pill' the night before.

YOU KNOW YOU'RE A MANEATER WHEN . . .

Group sex is having it off with the whole of *Westlife*.

YOU KNOW YOU'RE A MANEATER WHEN . . .

You were one of the first people to buy a vibrating phone. No wonder you asked for the largest one in the shop.

YOU KNOW YOU'RE A MANEATER WHEN . . .

You went for a job as a bartender. You thought the advert wanted someone who was "good at pulling pants".

YOU KNOW YOU'RE A MANEATER WHEN . . .

You orgasm so much that you have to fake a state of non-arousal (for solemn occasions like job interviews, family dinners and funerals).

YOU KNOW YOU'RE A MANEATER WHEN . . .

You were hired as consultant for Sharon Stone's role in *Basic Instinct*, but they had to tone your suggestions down.

YOU KNOW YOU'RE A MANEATER WHEN . . .

You can't help your John Wayne swagger.

YOU KNOW YOU'RE A MANEATER WHEN . . .

Your doctor has created a special DIY smear test kit for you because a) you take up too much of his time and b) he's scared what he might find up there.

YOU KNOW YOU'RE A MANEATER WHEN . . .

You have A, B, C, D, E, F and G spots.

YOU KNOW YOU'RE A MANEATER WHEN . . .

Foreplay is like cooking: why waste time dressing a cucumber when there are meals you can shove straight in the oven?

YOU KNOW YOU'RE A MANEATER WHEN . . .

You offer cruise holidays in your birth canal.

YOU KNOW YOU'RE A MANEATER WHEN . . .

Only qualified sub-mariners emerge unscathed.

YOU KNOW YOU'RE A MANEATER WHEN . . .

You don't give out your business card in meetings...you leave them in public phone boxes.

YOU KNOW YOU'RE A MANEATER WHEN . . .

You no longer find those 'Y-shaped coffin' jokes amusing. (Actually, it'll be more of a 'T' if you carry on like this.)

YOU KNOW YOU'RE A MANEATER WHEN . . .

You regret your early decision to tattoo boyfriends' names on your body. You have so many now that when naked you look more like a war memorial.

YOU KNOW YOU'RE A MANEATER WHEN . . .

You have shares in the pharmaceutical company that produces *KY Jelly*.

YOU KNOW YOU'RE A MANEATER WHEN . . .

You join the RAC to guarantee a good servicing whenever you have a breakdown.

YOU KNOW YOU'RE A MANEATER WHEN . . .

Your bikini line is hairless after unwittingly flossing a hundred men's molars.

YOU KNOW YOU'RE A MANEATER WHEN . . .

Your phone number is an 0898 number.

YOU KNOW YOU'RE A MANEATER WHEN . . .

Your love life is too shocking for *Jerry Springer*.

YOU KNOW YOU'RE A MANEATER WHEN . . .

Your telephone number isn't
listed in the phone book,
but in the back of
The Sunday Sport.

YOU KNOW YOU'RE A MANEATER WHEN . . .

Men need an HGV licence before they can handle your boobs.

YOU KNOW YOU'RE A MANEATER WHEN . . .

And a dangerous weapons licence before they venture as far as your knickers.

YOU KNOW YOU'RE A MANEATER WHEN . . .

You always turn the light on after sex by opening the car door.

YOU KNOW YOU'RE A MANEATER WHEN . . .

People say you're 'open' and they're not referring to your personality. You're still flattered.

YOU KNOW YOU'RE A MANEATER WHEN . . .

The men's pubes in your bed could re-string The Philharmonic's violin section.

YOU KNOW YOU'RE A MANEATER WHEN . . .

You are looking forward to retirement age – you'll have more time for your hobby.

YOU KNOW YOU'RE A MANEATER WHEN . . .

You've invented a quick-release system for your bras to save men time.

YOU KNOW YOU'RE A MANEATER WHEN . . .

Your libido, if harnessed, could replace 3 nuclear power stations.

YOU KNOW YOU'RE A MANEATER WHEN . . .

You do a lot for charity – your annual 'Shagathons' are legendary.

YOU KNOW YOU'RE A MANEATER WHEN . . .

You spend most of your holidays on your back / front / knees / up against a wall. Please tick applicable.

YOU KNOW YOU'RE A MANEATER WHEN . . .

Blow-up dolls are modelled on you.

YOU KNOW YOU'RE A MANEATER WHEN . . .

Your mouth is always open in an 'o' shape.

YOU KNOW YOU'RE A MANEATER WHEN . . .

You've done it doggy style more often than the randiest of Collies.

YOU KNOW YOU'RE A MANEATER WHEN . . .

Your pelvic muscles are in training for the Olympics.

YOU KNOW YOU'RE A MANEATER WHEN . . .

You own an A-Z of your erogenous zones.

YOU KNOW YOU'RE A MANEATER WHEN . . .

You lost your virginity to several men. No, really.

YOU KNOW YOU'RE A MANEATER WHEN . . .

You're so strong that people often say you are built like a fortress. Funny how your portcullis is never shut. And your moat is overflowing.

YOU KNOW YOU'RE A MANEATER WHEN . . .

Your idea of house cleaning is a quick change of the sheets, flush the old condoms down the loo and, next please!

YOU KNOW YOU'RE A MANEATER WHEN . . .

You're more flexible than the most complicated example of origami.

YOU KNOW YOU'RE A MANEATER WHEN . . .

A fairy god-mother refuses to grant your wish on grounds of taste and decency.

YOU KNOW YOU'RE A MANEATER WHEN . . .

You have a list of instructions tattooed on your inner thigh.

YOU KNOW YOU'RE A MANEATER WHEN . . .

It will be your fault if mankind dies out – you'll have eaten them all.

YOU KNOW YOU'RE A MANEATER WHEN . . .

From an early age you knew you wanted to be a model...for life drawing classes.

YOU KNOW YOU'RE A MANEATER WHEN . . .

You curb your calorific intake by occasionally spitting, not swallowing.

YOU KNOW YOU'RE A MANEATER WHEN . . .

Your first words in the morning are 'pleased to meet you – my name's...'.

YOU KNOW YOU'RE A MANEATER WHEN . . .

All the hotels in your area charge their rooms out to you by the hour. You charge yourself out by the minute.

YOU KNOW YOU'RE A MANEATER WHEN . . .

Your oestrogen levels are so high that, when you give blood, the vials are immediately transferred to the HRT clinic.

YOU KNOW YOU'RE A MANEATER WHEN . . .

You didn't bother watching *Debbie Does Dallas* because there wasn't enough sex in it.

YOU KNOW YOU'RE A MANEATER WHEN . . .

A Black Widow spider's bedside manner is less predatory than yours.

YOU KNOW YOU'RE A MANEATER WHEN . . .

Your idea of a low fat spread is skinny legs.

YOU KNOW YOU'RE A MANEATER WHEN . . .

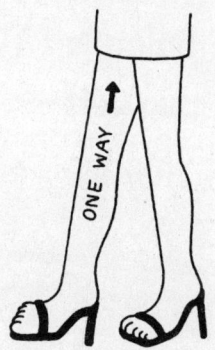

YOU KNOW YOU'RE A MANEATER WHEN . . .

You have a well balanced diet – meat and two veg is always on your menu.

YOU KNOW YOU'RE A MANEATER WHEN . . .

Anything less than a threesome is dull.

YOU KNOW YOU'RE A MANEATER WHEN . . .

Your favourite wine is 'yes, yes, yes!'.

YOU KNOW YOU'RE A MANEATER WHEN . . .

YOU KNOW YOU'RE A MANEATER WHEN . . .

You've had more rides than Disney World.

YOU KNOW YOU'RE A MANEATER WHEN . . .

You visit an Internet chat-room and virtually sleep with every man in it.

YOU KNOW YOU'RE A MANEATER WHEN . . .

Your definition of erotic is talking whilst you make love...not to your lover, but to the taxi-driver taking you home.

YOU KNOW YOU'RE A MANEATER WHEN . . .

You have timeshare lovers all over the world.

YOU KNOW YOU'RE A MANEATER WHEN . . .

You are a lady of the night - and day. Actually, any time will do.

YOU KNOW YOU'RE A MANEATER WHEN . . .

Romance is...oh, forget it.

YOU KNOW YOU'RE A MANEATER WHEN . . .

Cynthia Paine could learn a thing or two from you.

For the latest humour books from Summersdale, check out

www.summersdale.com